Monica: pour toute éternité, l'amour de ma vie

Monica: for all eternity, the love of my life

by
Alan Beausoleil

authorHOUSE™

1663 LIBERTY DRIVE, SUITE 200
BLOOMINGTON, INDIANA 47403
(800) 839-8640
WWW.AUTHORHOUSE.COM

© 2005 Alan Beausoleil. All Rights Reserved.

No part of this book may be reproduced, stored in a retrieval system, or transmitted by any means without the written permission of the author.

First published by AuthorHouse 10/18/05

ISBN: 1-4208-8184-1 (sc)

Printed in the United States of America
Bloomington, Indiana

This book is printed on acid-free paper.

Photographs taken by Mrs. Tina Dunn

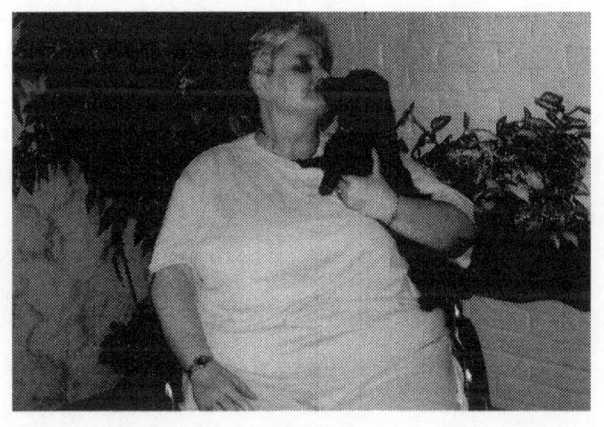

Monica: pour toute éternité, l'amour de ma vie.
Monica: for all eternity, the love of my life.

Preface

After writing the following book I began to feel that some explanation was needed on the subject of marriage and pre-marital sex. Successful marriages are built on good solid character. Many lost people have enough good solid character to have a lasting relationship. A lot of born-again believers who are not serious about their walk with God, don't. Marriage is a lot like dancing, (oops, we Baptists don't believe in dancing.) Anyway, the male partner is supposed to lead and the female is to follow his cues. As they move in harmony to become better dancers, they have to be more sensitive to their partners lead. Marriage is an ever-changing relationship as people mature. Pre-marital sex worked for us because we both had good, sound character. Honor and dignity meant something to me.

I was asked why we just didn't get married when we fell in love and decided to express our love in a physical manner. We were both 17. The answer to that question is truly tragic. We both knew what the answer would have been: "You're too young." My parents were about 30 when they married. If they had 5 years of happiness it would surprise me. All they did was fight. It was just easier to let Monica become pregnant. There would be no argument about us getting married then. The point is: Parents, listen to your children. They want to talk to you. Just listen.

Many parents listen to their kids and proceed to ignore what they have heard and superimpose their own wishes and desires into their children's lives instead. Parents should guide their children instead of force-feeding them a pre-written script. Listening is becoming a lost art to many married people. Talking to your mate is not supposed to be a shouting match. There are no scorekeepers. Just listen. Try to understand what you are being told. Sometimes you have to read between the lines. What is wrong dear? Something is bothering her and she is unable to put it into words. Keep asking until you get to the root of the problem. Maybe "I'm sorry" and a hug is all that's needed. Divorce Court is much more expensive.

May all of your marriages grow stronger every day. Trust me, there is nothing more comforting to a man than a wife who is in love with her husband. Men, it is well worth the time and effort.

-Bro Al

Introduction

My name is Alan Beausoleil. The people at the church I go to call me Bro Al, because when I taught Sunday School I didn't think the kids could say Beausoleil, so I told them to call me Bro Al. I was wrong. Our current Pastor's 2-year-old daughter can say it, and ever-so-sweetly. I decided to write my story simply because my current situation is so sad I thought it might be therapeutic. Although this is not a love story it is about love. Love, that's what makes life worth living. We often confuse it with lust, and often abuse it. Some people go from one mate to another seeking love only to be disappointed. They, unfortunately, have believed what the devil and Hollywood have had to say about love. The truth of the matter is that love comes from God. He gave it to us to hold our marriages together when times get tough. Things like honor and strength of character are the backbone of love. People without these qualities soon find themselves in Divorce Court.

Chapter One

My story starts out at the age of 17 when I met my future wife. I was the kind of boy that chased after the girls instead of running from them. When I was in the 2nd grade I walked a girl home from school everyday. When we got to her house we would sit on a glider in her back yard and hold hands and kiss. Life was great. At least it was until my family moved out of town. They never asked me what I wanted. I don't believe they even cared. For some time after that I believed I had an invisible alligator under the basement stair. Guess they thought I was loony tunes. I never told them the truth. Why should I? They would never have believed me anyway.

In my teen years, I enjoyed dancing and going to parties and doing all the things Baptists say you are not supposed to do. Although I had chased after girls from a very early age, I had never really caught one. That was about to change very soon. The girl I met that fateful day was named Monica Marie. Boy did she look good. Umm, umm, umm. She wore a navy blue top trimmed in white that was stretched to the breaking point across her chest. Love at first sight? No. But I was definitely interested. She was, in fact, the girl next door. Everyone has heard about the girl next door, but I had found her. My parents had recently been divorced and my father and I had just moved into a ramshackle house on ten acres. I first saw Monica as I was raking leaves, on a balmy day in December.

"Hi, How are ya? My name is Alan." (*Be careful, you don't want to mess this up.*) It turned out she was a day older than I, but because I had skipped a grade, she was in high school and I was a freshman at Wayne State University in Detroit, Michigan. She was impressed and I was beginning to feel lucky. "Wanna go out on a date???" (*We could go to a movie followed by a couple of hours on lovers and lane and steam up the car windows.*) The question got asked, but the rest stayed in my head. She was beginning to look better all the time. I got to meet her parents that day. Her father, Ben, was a hardworking man who worked at many different jobs to support his family. At that time, he was working at Criss Craft building boats and running a fruit market. Her mother was, well…a very poor judge of character. I was, in fact, loaded with male hormones and needed no encouragement from anyone and she would turn out to play cupid. Oh well, c'est la vie.

We started keeping steady company on the weekends as I went to college Monday through Friday and worked part time to pay for it. I had no financial help from anyone. Back then it was possible to do that. Now college is much more expensive. At school, almost every building had an area with chairs and tables where you could study, or just watch the girls. In the summer or spring, the frat boys were busy throwing the sorority sisters into the nearest moat or pool of water. It was great entertainment. There is just something about a girl in a wet blouse. Anyway, our dating got a little more intense. We were in the habit of watching TV until the test pattern came on about 12:00 midnight or 1:00 a.m. (It didn't matter, we weren't watching it anyway.) She was all the entertainment I wanted. It was Bud Abbott who said "Who's on 1st". Well, I was. And heading to 2nd. I thought she was beautiful in the blue top with the white trim. I was to soon discover she looked even better without it. 40 years later, I still feel the same way. The only difference is that now she is in a nursing home and we have to put a "Do Not Disturb" sign on the door. We can hear the traffic in the hallway increase as time goes by. Yesterday, I heard someone say "I wonder how long they're gonna be this time???" She says I'm giving her a bad reputation. Guess you'd better learn to live with it.

Getting back to the story. At some point, I finally made it all the way around the bases. I guess you could say I had scored. It was a great victory. I couldn't have done it without my coach. Let me explain. My mother was deeply troubled about something. I thought it was from the trauma of the divorce, which didn't make sense because she was the cause of it. She didn't understand the husband is supposed to be the head of the house and that her part was to be submissive. One flesh didn't mean much to her and her brothers and sisters meant more to her than did her own husband. Now my father, on the other hand, obviously was reading the "Mister Roger's Sex Manual". It's a mystery to me how I was ever conceived. As impassionate as they were, I was the opposite. I turned out very passionate and romantic. When we came to visit my mother in Warren, Michigan, (a long way from Mansfield, Ohio), my wife and I would camp out on the floor. There was no spare bedroom and we invariably did a reenactment of the consummation of our marriage. One morning my mother said, "Do you have to do that *every* night?" She must have been listening very carefully because except for a couple of grunts and a sigh of relief, we were very quiet.

I looked at her and said "Yes. Yes we do." She was troubled, so I got sent to a shrink: Dr. Pierce, good name for a sex therapist, I'd say. Dr. Pierce gave me answers to my sexual questions that were helpful and true. A lot better than the fairy tales my father was feeding me. The neighborhood boys had laughed me to scorn.

Soon after my initial score and victory, I knocked on the back door of Monica's house on a Saturday morning. Her mother came to the door, obviously disturbed at being awakened before 12 noon. "What do you want?" She asked.

"I've come to see Monica", I said. She told me to go upstairs and wake her up. Are you serious??? You must be joking; you can't mean that. Sooooo, up I went. I found her in a long flannel nightgown, toasty warm. When I kissed her, she clung to my neck tightly. What else could I do? After slipping out of my clothes, I climbed in bed with her. After that, I never bothered to

Monica: pour toute éternité, l'amour de ma vie.

knock again. Would you believe they acted surprised when she became pregnant?

Chapter Two

Now, if you are a teen or young person reading this, don't let your parents catch you. They will probably take it away. Here is a newsflash for you: Don't expect the girls or ladies in your life to act rationally at all times. It just doesn't happen that way. Why?? I can't answer that. I haven't figured it out yet. Monica and I got to the point that we couldn't decide where to go on our dates. She didn't want to go anywhere I suggested but couldn't come up with any of her own. So I came up with Plan "B". Plan "B" involved a girl named Elise. Elise went to an all-girls school, Dominican, I think. I should have known she was a little odd; her father had painted his refrigerator pink. Now who in their right mind does that?? Getting kissed by that girl was like being attacked by a lamprey eel: a completely unique experience. When she started to get really excited, she would get out of the car and walk around it. I should have drove off and left her. She wanted me to take her for a drive in the country and see where I lived. But we

Alan Beausoleil

might run into the girl who lives next door. She was looking for trouble. I figured it might do some good for the two of then to meet. Sooo…. Off we went. 80 miles later we arrived to see Monica washing her car. She almost washed us. Monica was very hurt and I had accomplished what I set out to do: namely, to get rid of her attitude problem. The next week, I took Elise to her prom and gave her the bad news. She cried and cried. I didn't have the heart to tell her that she had walked around the car once too often. Funny thing is, years later, after Monica and I had had two kids, Elise became our closest friend. For the life of me, I can't remember how that happened. She even went camping with us and slept in the same tent and Monica and I and our boys and all done in good taste. She became like a sister.

One night while camping up North we left the kids with her and Monica and I went skinny dipping down the road a piece. Skinny dipping is swimming naked under the moonlight. Remember Adam and Eve? They did it all the time. I did say I was passionate and romantic, didn't I? Yeah, we did that too. Life was good that night.

Young people, I want to tell you something. Just when you feel good about life, something will come along and turn it upside down.

Chapter Three – The Curse

When we finally did get married, Monica was just a little pregnant. There is no such thing as being a little pregnant, you either is or you ain't. Our first born son was named David and he was the apple of my eye. The 2nd was named Peter. And he was the worm. They were about 3 years apart. Monica knows their birthdays; I don't. It wasn't long before it became apparent that they weren't walking right. Our doctor suggested we have them checked out at an Muscular Dystrophy clinic to see what they had. I don't think he had the stomach to tell us what he feared. They had a whole team of doctors, nurses and therapists to give you the impression that they could help you. Truth was, they couldn't do a thing to help. Duchenne Muscular Dystrophy: A death sentence. From that day on, I knew what the end of the story was going to be. At least when a man faces the firing squad, he is blindfolded so he can't see it coming and it's quick. MD provides neither. I cried and cried and cried. As I sit and write this, the tears are streaming down my cheeks. Yesterday, we were informed that the nursing home is going to close down the wing my wife's room is in (MD has taken her ability to walk). The happiness we found for a brief 2 weeks looks as if it will fade away also. My Pastor tells me that "all things work together for good to them that love God." So does my Bible. I guess my tears and pain are obscuring the truth I know is there. I really wish he'd take my life and get it over with.

You will recall I said this story is about love. God loves us. He allowed his son Jesus to die for our sins. True love is not the lustful love Monica and I started out with, but the *agape* love that developed. See, when we were doing all that fun stuff – and I've only written about a small portion of it – we were both Episcopalians. At that time, they didn't seem to care what we did. When our boys were small, we allowed the loco, I mean local, Baptist Church to take them to Sunday School on the bus. We were both searching for answers to the burning question: "Why did all of our children have to have a disease that would soon kill them?" We soon attended a couple Sundays. One Saturday, the bus worker, who was also the Assistant Pastor's wife, told my wife, about how Jesus loved her and died on the cross so she could go to heaven instead of hell. Monica kneeled, prayed and asked Jesus to forgive her sins and save her. I wasn't home. Now the Pastor of the First Baptist Church of Clio was named Clytee Harnes. Sounded like some kind of rig that belonged on a horse. When he preached he would blow himself up like a bagpipe. His style was, to say the least, unique. He caught me home one summer day. As we sat in a couple of lawn chairs in the back yard, I remember there was a pine tree and the grape arbor nearby, he told me about Jesus and answered my questions. I, too, got saved. But I still had no answer to the question "Why?" Why did my boys have this horrible disease? 30 years later, I still don't have the answer. Not once in our entire married life did I ever blame my wife or allow her to blame herself for the defective genes that she had and passed on to our sons. I loved her too much for that.

Raising handicapped children is a difficult and heartbreaking job. Can you imagine how a mother's heart can break watching her handicapped son struggling to walk to school, knowing how easy it would be for him to fall. "I'm a big boy now, mama, I can do this." He refused any help. Four years later, he would be in a wheelchair.

One friend expressed the opinion that God knew he could trust us with such a responsibility. Well, it was a responsibility I never wanted. One normal child would have been nice. Some people who have normal children take the health of their children for granted. It is not at all uncommon to hear about child abuse on the evening news, or a child being sexually molested by some member of the family. My two boys would eventually be taken by a disease while others were throwing theirs away. It doesn't seem right. It is good that only God can see inside our hearts and minds. One Sunday morning, on the way to church, that same boy told me: "I have a stomachache."

"So, what?" You can see how compassionate I was.

Five minutes later: "Daddy, I really hurt".

Now I knew we had a problem. You've got two choices: 1) We will see the Doctor tomorrow or 2) To the ER right now. "If it's all the same to you I'd just as soon go to the ER right now." So, off to the hospital we went. When we got there we sat and waited. A nurse came out after a while, a long while, and looked at David.

"We'd better take an x-ray", she said, and left, pushing his wheelchair down a hallway. They came back soon after with consent forms for the emergency surgery that was necessary.

Monica went with David as they prepared him for surgery. While they were putting tubes down his throat, he said: "Sit me up, I can't breathe". Those were his last words that I know of. His heart stopped and he turned blue. Monica told one nurse: "Call my Pastor and call him now.". The Pastor was in the midst of teaching Sunday School, but he picked a replacement for Sunday School and his Pulpit and came immediately. This was Bro Carl Petty; we had changed churches. About an hour later, a Doctor came to us, took us to a small room and matter-of-factly told us our son was dead. Our 13 year-old son was dead. He was the apple of my eye. Gone! Mike Tyson or Mohammed Ali could not have hit me any harder than that news.

Six months later, my wife flipped out and spent some time in the hospital. "Why me, Lord?" I was conducting the junior church at our West Side Baptist Church in Corrona, Michigan. "Why me? Why". As sad as it seems, this was only the beginning of our sorrows. 25 years has passed and it still hurts me to

Monica: pour toute éternité, l'amour de ma vie.

talk about it. We still had one son left and his time was coming.

Chapter Four – Peter

Peter deserves a chapter all his own. David was the apple of my eye. Peter was the worm. Peter got 90% of all the spankings and deserved every one. My father used to tell me when I was about to get spanked: "This is going to hurt me more than you". Crap! "You've got it coming and I intend to enjoy every minute of it", is what I told my boys. Peter was a good baby, hardly ever cried. Maybe he was just building up steam. Our 1st confrontation came when he was too young to spank. He would get up during the night, go to the refrigerator and finger paint with the jelly all over. When Monica woke up to this mess, she wasn't happy at all. I soon decided this little gangster wasn't going to get the best of me. After all, I was the head of the house, master of all the eye could see, and so on. What was needed was a plan. Yes, we needed a plan. It took a while, but it turned out to be a stroke of genius. The plan, as it turned out, suited my personality to a tee. I intended to scare him. Every parent with small kids does it all the time. You hide and when they coming looking for you, you jump out of hiding and roar like a lion and watch their little legs carry them away, giggling all the way. But this had to be special! I assembled the following equipment: an amplifier, microphone and some wire and, oh yes, a speaker. This took place some 35 years ago when these things were not as common as today. The microphone and amplifier went in the basement. The speaker went in the frig. The wire connected the both of them. The plan was for Monica to send Peter to the frig on an errand to help Mommy. When Peter got to the frig, she was to stomp on the floor 3 times. My part was to turn on the amp and roar into the mic. The amplifier was already turned wide open. It worked perfectly. I scared him so bad he never got in it again at night. In fact, he would not walk past the frig. without looking at it at all times. I later moved the speaker to the kitchen wall near the ceiling where I could talk to my wife while in the basement. What made it perfect was that she couldn't talk to me. It had worked so well the first time, I decided to do it again. Monica was feeding Peter some peas while he was in his high chair. When I growled this time he spit a mouthful of peas at her and jumped clean out of the high chair. I was told never to do that again. I didn't. But that does not stop me from howling with laughter every time I recall those events.

Why is one child so good while the next one so bad??? I don't know. When I was 17, I thought I knew everything. I could tell you if you had asked me. The Bible says pride goeth before a fall. This, I can tell you for sure: God knows how to deal with pride and all the rest of our sins. The man who has wisdom will love him for it. I'm thankful for the Holy Spirit and the privilege of prayer. There is nothing sweeter than a prayer partner. Someone you can share the "heart-ache and the 1000 natural shocks the flesh is heir to" with. Take them to God's throne with tears streaming down your face. On the other hand, the fool knows none of this. The only way to go through life is to be secure in the knowledge that Jesus is indeed your savior. His grace not only saves us, but also keeps us saved and sustains us in our daily walk. The quote comes from Shakespeare's play, Hamlet. Hamlet was considering suicide when he spoke those words.

Getting back to Peter. I don't know what inspired him to wage war on me, but wage war he did. These Doctors that warn us not to break the child's spirit are full of it. Our battle would take us to the breaking point. It would come to the point that I would throw him into a cold snow bank not wanting him back at all! "Get our and stay out" I yelled, and slammed the door. Well, I guess we need to go back to the start of the war. Everybody seems to be interested in sex: how to be a better lover, the best techniques and so on. Not near as much interest is shown in how to raise a child. I freely admit that the act of conception is clearly the most pleasurable part. To provide for my family, I had to work. If I worked overtime it paid time and a half or double time. The wages were good. For this, I was thankful to my employer General Motors. Being gone much of the time left my wife to care for the children. Being somewhat old-fashioned, I preferred it that way. Many young people today don't have that option. It takes two paychecks to provide food and shelter. The elimination of the middle class today in America is being ignored by a lot of people. Let me get back to the war started by Peter before my book turns into a rant. I began to notice odd things happening. Sometimes, I couldn't find some tool I needed. He's been gone from the house quite some time and I still can't find things. But when sand found its way into my oil can that had a squirt trigger, I needed a better explanation. Some metal rods were removed from my file cabinet and bent into pretzels. Various other things began to happen which I don't recall. But the straw that broke the camel's back was when someone broke the copper feed line that supplied gas to the hot water heater. We had just come back from a Muscular Dystrophy sponsored bowling event which lasted about 4 to 5 hours and the house reeked of gas! The first thing I checked was the pilot lights on the stove. All were lit. The family, meanwhile, was standing out in the cold and snow. In the basement, I found the furnace functioning properly. As I turned to inspect the water heater, I couldn't believe what I saw. The supply line was dangling freely with evidence that it had been moved back and forth until the metal fatigued and gave way. There was a shutoff right there, but I couldn't see it knowing that the house could explode at any minute. The mind does not work properly in times of peril. I grabbed a wrench and turned the gas off outside at the meter, and opened all the doors and windows, returning the house to a condition of safety. David was wheelchair-bound and couldn't get in the basement. They had no friends over at the time. Everything pointed to Peter. I beat him until I was out of breath. I definitely stepped over the line. When I regained my breath; I beat him again and then threw him out onto a snow bank. I was furious and out of control. I did not know what to do with him. Monica said I had to let him back in the house. "Let 'em freeze!" I did throw him a coat. What to do now??? It didn't take the devil long to attack us as we, as new Christians, were starting to be involved with the church. Maybe we can give him to the Pastor? I clearly didn't want my own son in my house. When I told the Pastor if he didn't take him I was gonna kill him, he agreed. He meant temporarily and I thought I was rid of him for good. Three days later, the Assistant Pastor called me up and said I had to take him back. Oh great! Just when my blood pressure was back to normal.

Did you counsel with Peter? Yes. Did he do it on purpose? Yes. Why? I don't think he is getting enough of your attention. Oh Good grief! Well, another plan was needed. No amplifier and speaker was going to work this time. This time, prayer was added to the planning process. As before I, with the guidance of the Holy Spirit, came up with a plan. Again it suited me to a tee. This little gangster who was now about 7 or 8 years old wasn't going to get the best of me. No, no, no. I was the head of the house and so on. I don't like problems or anything that brings turmoil into my home. Peter spoke not a word on the short way home, nor did I. The time I had available to be with my wife and family was in short supply. Every time I tried to do something with my boys, they would be watching TV and said come back later daddy, we are watching TV. In addition to being romantic and passionate I had a flare for the dramatic. Would you care to guess what the plan would be?? I should put it in a later chapter just to tease you. Not! That's an expression I picked up from the kids of today: Not! Maybe even Pinky and the Brain. My wife and I just loved that show. *Narf poit.* I even bought her a pinky doll. When she went in the nursing home she gave it away. There is untold joy in giving. Oh well.

Back to the plan. When we got back home, I brought everyone outside: Monica, David, Peter and Duffy. Duffy was our loyal dog. Of the whole bunch, the dog was the most cooperative. Then I brought the TV out and set it on a 5 foot snow bar. Next, I came out with my grandfather's shotgun. Grandfather didn't need it any more. He wasn't around. A cold glass of water would have been worth the price of a shotgun where he was now. You all pay attention, here. I then put 3 rounds of #6 birdshot into the TV, left it on the snow bank and went back in the house. Soon after, the family came in also.

Now anybody would assume that the trouble would be over. I had a chat with the gangster just to be on the safe side. I told him that if anything of mine was destroyed, I would start destroying his toys. Gretta Goose would be the first to go and he might find his bed out in the snow one day. Sure enough, he still had to test me. Peter loved Gretta Goose. He had bought her at a garage sale with his own money. So... I cut the head off of Gretta Goose and put it on his pillow, just like the scene from *The Godfather*. Peter never said anything about it.

After a week I was dying with curiosity, so I asked him: "Where is Gretta Goose?"

"You cut the head off her", he answered.

"Do you know why?" I asked.

"Yes."

"Is there going to be any more trouble"

"No."

Two weeks later, he got saved at revival services at the First Baptist Church of Clio, our first church. Not one tear did Peter let me see. Not one. Years later, Monica told me he cried his eyes out over that goose. That boy had grit that he never got from me. I don't know where he got it. I would like to say I won all the battles and wars with Peter, but he won once. Just once. I count myself lucky to have that good of a record against such an adversary. Peter had character of his own, different from mine, but nevertheless, character.

I might add that we had no TV for at least 5 years. It made my father quite mad. *C'est la vie, mon Pere.* There was an immediate improvement in our boys' school grades. Parents, never give in to your children and let them rule you. A spoiled child is no good to himself or anyone else.

My job moved to Ohio and so did I. I was surprised to hear much anti-Michigan sentiment when I got here. I expected it from the guys in the shop. Afterall, I did go ahead of some of them in seniority. But not on the news, from people everywhere, and especially not from the pulpit. I never expected to read about football fans throwing dog bones at opposing players. Except the things just mentioned, I found the people of Ohio to be friendly and kind.

Peter made it to high school. He also grew in size as my wife Monica's strength was ebbing from her body just as had happened with the kids. We tried to ignore it and every time we were jolted back to reality by evidence of her slow but steady decline in health. It was an occasion for much grief, sorrow and tears. So many tears. Why did we have to suffer so much??? Our love, which started out to be so tender, true and extremely exciting, was being tempered by adversity. It survived. Peter was becoming more than Monica could physically handle. She had, by taking such excellent care of him, spoiled him. When I tried to help take care of him, he became demanding beyond my endurance – a characteristic which would destroy his future marriage. About this time we found out that our insurance company would allow us to convert hospital days of stay into a dollar amount to pay for home health care. So... We started getting some help taking care of Peter. One day the aide the agency sent over put a latex glove on her head, covering her nose, and blew it up by breathing in her mouth and out her nose. It made her look like a chicken. Monica laughed so hard she actually fell on the floor. Another aide showed up dressed like a pirate. Again, she cracked up. I, unfortunately, missed this by being at work. Another aide by the name of Ann Sanney took care of Peter for a time, and had a son named James who is today the Pastor of the church I attend. Small world isn't it. God weaves together the threads of our lives to make a patchwork quilt we are not allowed to see until a later date. Is not God Great! After much trial and tribulation, Peter graduated from Malabar High School.

We were able to place him at a place called Echoing Hills when he turned 18 and was eligible for Social Security. It happened in the nick of time, as taking care of Peter had almost killed Monica.

Echoing Hills was run by Christian people and was a ministry for them. They had a summer camp for handicapped kids that was as good as it gets. A-class. Every holiday we always went to visit Peter. They would put a whole turkey on the table just for us. What a treat! The doors at Echoing Hills were all operated by electric eyes, so that anyone could come or go as they pleased. Peter would get a hold of some stinky bait and go fishing when he wanted. Also, any critter that wanted in got in. One day a large black lab got in. Now black labs seldom walk anywhere, they always run. They seem to have too much energy. One day, on a holiday I think but I don't know for certain, while Betsy was doing dishes, this black lab ran right between her legs at full speed. Whatever she had in her hands was thrown in the air and she screamed with all she had. I saw the dog come racing out of the kitchen and out the door in a flash. I laughed and laughed. You can always tell when you have had a good laugh: your stomach hurts and you come close to wetting your britches. My housekeeper is a treat to watch as she encounters a spider, especially a big black hairy one. The spider is doomed. The first thing you see or hear is the scream. She has been known to beat the spider to death with a shoe when she caught up with it. It's like a "Tom & Jerry" cartoon as she pursues the spider and sometimes she yells at him while chasing him. I've bought a rubber spider just for the fun of it, but it only worked once. She catches on quick.

Now ole Peter always had plenty of spending cash. When my mother died she wanted to leave Peter something, which would disqualify him from Social Security. She made arrangements with someone close to take care of this. These arrangements were soon forgotten. People get funny when it comes to money. So, I set aside a small insurance policy which named me as beneficiary for Peter. As a result, the people at Echoing Hills thought he was wealthy. At least one nurse did, stupid woman. She went into his room one night and seduced him. Peter wasn't able to perform any type of sexual intercourse. He was obviously able to be the recipient of oral sex. Guess what? He liked it and wanted more of it. His father understood completely. Poor Peter, he just wanted his part of the American Dream. He was determined to get married. Getting married meant that he couldn't stay at Echoing Hills. He had to give up his security for a shot at happiness. All that any parent wants for their kids is for them to be happy. Well, most parents do. Knowing that this was not going to turn out well makes it hurt all the more. I guess it was crying time again. They got married. She wanted a big wedding. In consideration, she had a grandchild (she must have been an old hand at all of this.) I told Peter, "No matter how bad it gets, don't call home. Your mother and I have done all we can for you. You're on your own." After a while his wife left him. He got some help from social services but was alone for long periods of time. He ended up in the hospital with pneumonia. The last two years of his life were

Monica: pour toute éternité, l'amour de ma vie.

spent at an extended care wing of the Coshocton County Hospital on a ventilator. He died Christmas Eve, 1997. Just 18 minutes short of Christmas Day. Christmas has not been a happy time for Monica and me ever since. Two down and one to go. Her time was coming and we both knew it. There was just no end to the sorrow and grief. Still, no answer to the burning question: Why? Why us? Today we are both DNR status. DNR means Do Not Resuscitate.

Every time you get brought to your knees you try to get up again. We had time to try to rebuild our relationship. Trouble was that physically we both were not in good shape. Just before Peter died, I was in the Emergency Room. They said I had Pulmonary Edema and gave me a lasix and said I would soon pee. They were right, two urinals full. Well, we will soon start the final chapter of this sad tale.

Chapter 5 – The Nursing Home

This is going to be the hardest chapter to write. The pain is still fresh and my heart is like a festering wound. October 27, 2004 my wife just could not get up out of her chair. She tried and tried. Even when she could still get up, it was pitiful to see her walk. But she kept on keeping on. When she reached the end of the line, it crushed me. About the same time, my foot doctor informed me I had another ulcer on my right foot. This had happened two years before and had taken all winter to heal. I had hit rock bottom. Or so I thought. The struggle to put one foot in front of the other was more than I could do. The solitude of the 4 bedroom house gave me time to recall all past pain, which came back to haunt me. It was a very hard winter. I have a bipap machine which requires electricity to help me breath at night and we were without power for 5 days because of an ice storm. I survived, but my shortness of breath got worse. The only good thing I could see at that time was the revelation of the three neighbors that I received help from. My foot needed daily dressing changes. The lady right next door was a cardiac technician who had lupus and a bone disease. Some days I think she dressed my foot while she was in pain herself. I have an account with the local florist. I send my wife a new bouquet every week. She's the only one in the nursing home with a constant supply of fresh flowers. One day, I could tell the lady who was dressing my foot needed a little boost. So I called the florist and ordered some flowers for her. "Make sure you don't mess up the card. These flowers are for a married woman. Make it read: 'Thanks for the nursing care.'" A card saying with love would have gotten me in hot water in a New York minute. Later, she called me to thank me and she sounded like a schoolgirl, she was so happy. Flowers say a lot to a woman. Another neighbor, off to one side and in back of me, would fill-in in a pinch. The trouble is that their dog would try to steal anything she could get a hold of, including the bandage and gauze. This dog was a black lab and routinely ate coal. That's right, coal. I've never seen a dog eat coal before. Maybe that's why her coat was so black and shiny. From this neighbor, I could usually count on a hot cup of tea and maybe some cheese. I'm also a mooch. There is not a "Don't Feed the Bears" sign on my door! My nickname when I taught High School was Sugar Bear. I didn't drink tea before that. My housekeeper sure likes tea. She heads for the can (bathroom) as soon as she gets here. The last neighbor is a man who has shown me much concern and care. He is a successful business man and called me everyday when the power was out. He even cleaned up, or had someone clean up, downed tree limbs from the ice storm. This was no small task. I would like for these people to all come to know Jesus as I do from reading my book. I thank God for these three neighbors. I, of course, have one neighbor that wouldn't give a crippled crab a crutch. She is a member of a nearby Baptist church. Personally, I think she's not right in the head. But what do I know?

I looked everywhere for some relief from the depression I was in. It is interesting that my French calendar for two days ago included the phrase: *"avoir le cafard"* which is, literally translated, "to have the cockroach" or to be depressed. My depression bottomed out somewhere in January. Tina, my housekeeper, and I started sharing prayer requests and having prayer together before she started handling the destruction I had done the previous week. Trust me, I need a housekeeper. My wife and I have had many housekeepers over the last 20 years, but Tina is the best.

I like to sing and whistle which have both improved with time. Now that I was all alone (humanly speaking) I could sing to my heart's content at all hours of the day or night without bothering anyone. "What a Friend We Have in Jesus" and "Sweet Hour of Prayer" became favorites. As I began to sing, God's Holy Spirit would fill me and tears of joy came to me to comfort me in my darkest hours. I began to pray more, not mere lip service, but really pouring my heart out to God. As I began to read and study my Bible and sing a new appreciation of the truth it contained became more real and I began to understand what a privilege it is to talk directly to the Creator of All That Is.

Meanwhile, back at the ranch (that's an expression used in the early cowboy movies), Monica was experiencing difficulties of her own. She had people all around her. The trouble was that most of them weren't playing with a full deck. When she first came to Mansfield Memorial Homes she was scared and overwhelmed. They gave her one quarter of a small room which her roommate was monopolizing. She was, at the start, not well received. But when the nurses and aides saw what a sweet and loving spirit she had, their hearts began to melt. The separation we were going through began to take its toll and we started to talk about a private room as her roommate was being abusive and mean. One day, the roommate was rushed to the hospital with heart problems. All the personnel knew how sad and blue Monica had become and they conspired to give us some privacy. As I entered the room, the aide said to me: "Don't worry. I won't let anyone get through that door." What else could I do??? Now time, Diabetes and Muscular Dystrophy have taken their toll, but where there is a will, there is a way. We enjoyed ourselves together. When we came out we were both feeling much better and this event was the highlight of the activities calendar. You can't stop that many women from talking, not a chance. I called the florist and sent a bouquet of flowers to the head conspirator. I seem to be in the habit of sending flowers to express thanks. Soon after, Monica got a private room. Guess where I'm going tomorrow?

I'm not going to tell you everything is coming up roses, because it's not. Monica has developed some cardiac problems. When our son Peter was on a respirator for 2 years we vowed to never do that to each other. We are both DNR and have Living Wills. She is choosing to not allow a heart catheterization because she doesn't want to take the chance of getting stuck on life support systems. The viewpoint we both share.

At the start of this book I didn't know the answer to the question: Why? Why?? Why Us Lord?? I believe I now know the answer. The answer is this: These many years of pain, grief and suffering have prepared me to write this book. Two dead children and a beloved wife who could go at any time to write this book. Was it worth it? No! No! A thousand times, NO! I would have preferred to have healthy children any day. I did not have a choice. Writing the book was no problem. The actual writing was God's will which took about 12 days. I believe that this undertaking was the hand of God at work. I fully intend to sit back and want to see what he does next. Watching God at work is the most exciting think I can think of.

My personal prayer is that everyone that reads this book will develop a desire to become a born again Christian and walk as close to God as he or she possibly can.

> May God Bless You All,
> Brother Al

Alan Beausoleil

Molly

Molly, I'm so glad you're in my life.
You take out all the strife.

Molly, you are so sweet,
You make me want to get on my feet.

Molly so we could run
And have so much fun.

Molly, you like to speak
When you should sleep.

Molly you don't like to nap in your bed,
When you could run the halls instead.

Molly, God sent you as a special gift
That gives my life such a lift.

Molly, you are my speical friend,
I hope you're with me until the end.

- Monica Beausoleil

Note: Molly is a Dachshund

About the Author:

I graduated from Wayne State University in Detroit, Michigan with a B.S. degree in Industrial Education, although I spent most of my college years in the School of Engineering. Considering that my book is not technical at all, my education is not really relevant. What is important is that I lived the events that make up the book. Every tear talked about in the book rolled down my cheeks. Every sorrow and grief I bore. Not everybody gets healthy children. Our children had Duchenne Muscular Dystrophy. We raised them the best we could when they could no longer walk, we got wheelchairs for them. And we cried as they died.